THE
GOLDEN STATE

CLB 1610
© 1986 Illustrations and text: Colour Library Books Ltd.,
    Guildford, Surrey, England.
Text filmsetting by Acesetters Ltd., Richmond, Surrey, England.
All rights reserved.
1986 edition published by Arch Cape Press.
Printed in Spain.
ISBN 0 517 61394 8
h g f e d c b a
Dep. Leg. B-7.902-86

THE GOLDEN STATE

Text by
Lee Thomas

ARCH CAPE PRESS
New York

Ever since one wet January day in 1884, when a carpenter at John A. Sutter's Sawmill picked up a chunk of yellow metal and started one of history's great gold rushes, California has been to many the promised land; a land of unlimited opportunity.

People flocked to California in search of gold; they piled onto the railroads when the lines were fist pushed into California; they walked, drove and hitched into California when the citrus and grape industries called out for labor, when oil and natural gas were discovered, when Hollywood promised overnight stardom, when drought turned huge areas of the American southwest into a dust bowl, when shipyards and aircraft plants opened up thousands of new jobs.

In 1848 the population was estimated at 14,000; by the 1860s it was well on the way to half a million, and between 1860 and 1960 it doubled virtually every 20 years. California has long since overtaken New York as the most heavily populated member of the United States and is now approaching a figure of 20 million – roughly one in 20 of all Americans. By the year 2000 population pundits believe that that figure will have become one in five.

With this tremendous surge of manpower has come immense industrial muscle which, allied to the academic, artistic, scientific and commercial expertise attracted from around the world by unrivaled salaries and unsurpassed working conditions, has propelled California into a unique position: only five nations of the world produce and sell more goods than does this one American state, and one of those nations is the United States itself.

"California," says Michael Davie in his book, *In the Future Now*, "is the only society ever founded on respect for money, which is one reason why it is now the richest segment of the surface of the globe, and why Californians are the richest people there have ever been."

But even with the strength of its people, even with their highly successful "Work hard, play hard" philosophy, it is doubtful if California would have made such a mark on the world, or such wealth for its citizens, without its abundant natural attributes.

Its magnificent climate is certainly one. The coastal strip – roughly 2 percent of the state and where 94 percent of the people live – luxuriates in temperatures that rarely exceed 90 degrees Fahrenheit or fall to freezing point. Rainfall is moderate, about 20 inches a year in San Francisco, for instance. Yet north of that city there are areas that are deluged by as much as 180 inches a year. In the far south, summer temperatures in the desert areas hit Sahara heights, while the peaks of the Sierra Nevadas often experience temperatures as low as those of the Arctic.

The state's 158,000 square miles contain the impressive mountain ranges of the Sierra Nevada, as well as forests, deserts, lakes and 1,200 miles of the most beautiful coastal scenery to be seen anywhere, now protected by the extensive powers of a specially appointed Coastal Commission.

Within less than 100 miles of each other in California lie the highest and lowest points of the conterminous USA – Mt. Whitney at 14,494 feet, and Death Valley, 282 feet below sea level at its lowest point. The Valley was known to Red Indian tribes for generations, but was unknown to the white man until a party of prospectors seeking a shortcut to the gold fields stumbled upon it. It is now a national monument.

Mt. Whitney is part of the Sierra Nevada range that runs south for 430 miles from Lassen Peak to the fringes of Los Angeles. It is quite an experience for the first-time visitor to Los Angeles to drive along Melrose Avenue in temperatures of 80 degrees or more, while the snow capped peaks of the Sierras glint a dazzling white in the summer sky to the north.

High up in the Sierras, near the state border with Nevada, is one of the most beautiful of America's lakes, Lake Tahoe, more than 6,000 feet above sea level, nearly 200 square miles in area and, at a depth of 1,600 feet, one of the world's deepest. It is now a superbly developed resort area with Olympic standard skiing facilities, casinos, cabarets and nightclubs where the finest of America's entertainers regularly appear.

The state's main desert areas are the Colorado in the south west, where fewer than three inches of rain fall in a year and some of the world's highest temperatures have been recorded, and the Mojave Desert where, apart from a few military installations, aviation and rocket ranges and the occasional intrepid explorer, the desert's 25,000 square miles are as unsullied by human endeavor as on the day they were created.

California's forests, however, *have* suffered from the arrival of the settler. The redwood forests, for instance, where many of these magnificent trees are up to 2,000 years old and tower 300 feet, now cover less than 10 percent of their former territory. Recent, far-reaching state legislation ensures there will be no further inroads into one of California's great legacies.

The arrival of settlers, and the inevitable erosion of some of the state's natural beauty and riches, dates from the discovery of gold. But California's history, as far as the white man is concerned, goes back another century. The Spaniards can claim to have discovered California – then occupied by scattered Red Indian tribes – and, by the late 18th century, Franciscan friars were establishing missions along the Pacific coast, the first at San Diego in 1769. The Spaniards were eventually ousted by the Mexicans, leaving behind little more than their architecture and place names. In 1846 the emergent United States defeated Mexico, and huge tracts of land, including much of modern California, became American. In 1850 California became the 31st state of the Union.

At this time, of course, gold was still the major preoccupation of the State's immigrants; it had lured them into San Francisco by boat from all over Europe, as well as in more than 6,000 wagons on the hazardous overland trail from the Midwest and the East, on which cholera claimed more victims than hostile Indian tribes or extremes of climate and terrain.

Chinese faces became increasingly seen among the predominantly Anglo-Saxon workers and they stayed to form the origins of the Chinese communities in California today. Fifteen years later the railroads were dynamiting through the Rockies with the aid of hundreds of Irish laborers who also stayed on and, with the Italians and French, made San Francisco their new home.

The city had been founded only a century before, in 1776, when a landing was made in the bay by a Spanish expedition. Until California entered the Union, San Francisco was little more than a Spanish settlement, but in the 1830s the first American homes and ranches were established on the slopes of the 43 hills. With the gold rush all that changed, and the bay suddenly had to cope with vessels arriving daily from all parts. Wharves were hastily erected to cope with them; the hillsides suddenly sprouted tents and shanties, and the shrewder settlers opened up bars and gambling houses to part the prospectors from their golden gains.

Within ten years of the first find, San Francisco's 1845 population of about 300 had swelled to nearly 60,000, and the city had already established a character of its own. There was a Chinatown; North Beach was where the Italians set up home, and the Barbary Coast provided nightlife. There was also a commercial center and the peripheral services needed for the lifestyles spawned by the gold rush.

In the 1860s, oil replaced gold as the Californian bonanza and, until the end of the century, San Francisco's population and city development expanded fast. Then, in the course of a few minutes early in the morning of April 18, 1906, life as San Francisco knew it came to an end. An initial two-minute earthquake bowled over buildings and sparked off fires that raged for three days across the city, killing more than 500 people and, by destroying nearly 30,000 buildings, virtually razed the whole of the city's development.

As with the Great Fire of London, however, the disaster gave the City Fathers an opportunity to stamp out the unhygienic, cramped conditions caused by hasty, unplanned building and to reconstruct on far more generous lines. In less than 10 years the new San Francisco took shape, celebrated in 1915 by the Panama-Pacific Exposition.

As the 20th century progressed, the city's fine natural harbor ensured it became a major shipbuilder, mainly of naval craft, and many who came to work in the shipyards and allied industries as part of the war effort stayed on in San Francisco. Another expansion in population occurred after the opening in 1936 of the Oakland Bay Bridge, the eight and a quarter miles of which make it the longest steel bridge in the world. With two levels of traffic (replacing the ferry boat system across the Bay) it opened up the East Bay area into a major dormitory suburb of the city. More expansion followed in the 1960s with such elegant developments as the Golden Gateway and Ghirardelli Square near Fisherman's Wharf, one of the highlights on most visitors' itinerary.

San Franciscans like to think, with some justification, that their city provides a cultural oasis in the Californian social desert. Its museums include four devoted to the fine arts; Golden Gate Park houses the California Academy of Sciences; and specialist museums include wine, army and maritime exhibits, as well as institutions of local history such as Cable Bar Barn, the old U.S. Mint, and the Wells Fargo History Room.

It has its own symphony orchestra, opera and ballet companies, and offers a wide range of more contemporary music – jazz, ragtime and rock. And the many excellent ethnic restaurants reflect the cosmopolitan character of the city.

For 60 years San Francisco was the major Californian city, but, by the 1920s, it was being overtaken in size, and significance to the state economy, by its brash southern counterpart: Los Angeles. With around three million people, L.A. – as it is universally known – now has about four times the population of San Francisco. It was proclaimed by Father Crespi in 1769 when he accompanied the Spanish Expeditionary Force led by Gaspar de Portola. The first mission, San Gabriel, was founded there in 1771 and with the addition of another, San Fernando, the resulting settlement grew large enough to be considered the chief town of Mexican California.

The gold rush to the north altered the town's development and it became a rowdy cattle town until the Santa Fe railroad brought in new arrivals, many of them farmers from the Midwest who exploited the rich farming region. Within the five years or so of the railroad's arrival in 1885, the orange growing industry and the development of new towns around the central Los Angeles area saw the population increase to 50,000. By the turn of the century, with the discovery of oil and the opening up of port facilities at San Pedro, the population had more than doubled.

Individual communities such as Anaheim, Glendale, Santa Monica and Beverly Hills were absorbed, first by the advent of the automobile, then by further building development pulling them all together into one urban area, and with Hollywood established on the map Los Angeles emerged as the state's major city.

There are conflicting stories about how Hollywood came to be named. None can be proved, but one that seems as likely as any other is than an early English settler family, trying to recreate a little of their origins, planted holly trees in their garden. The climate put an end to the holly wood, but the name lived on.

Hollywood is now but an echo of the past. The film studios that remain are largely given over to television work. The area itself is a mosaic of office blocks, waste lots, hamburger stands, supermarkets, and second-class movie theaters. The domestic architecture is mock Spanish, mock Georgian, mock Gothic and mock Tyrolean, and the inhabitants seem to spend most of their leisure hours hosing the carefully manicured lawns that run straight down to the sidewalks. As Edward Thorpe writes in his book, *The Other Hollywood*, "Glamorous Hollywood is just the receding architectural hairline of the thirties, a fading generation frozen in the forties and fifties, and the young kids of today in the tatty cast-offs of various fashionable folk lores. Topographically it is fast becoming just a no-man's land between the business areas of downtown Los Angeles and the swank and plush areas of Beverly Hills and Bel Air." Sad, but true.

Since World War II, the city has continued to prosper, with leisure industries, aerospace, fashion and sport joining movies and TV as major employers and money earners for the city.

The Los Angeles Opera Company was founded in 1924, two years after the Hollywood Bowl was built for live outdoor performances of all kinds, from symphony concerts, the Beatles and Bob Dylan to political rallies. The city's prestigious Music Center was built in the 1960s and the several art galleries include the Norton Simon and J. Paul Getty museums. There is the Museum of Science and Industry at Exposition Park and the Hall of Science and Travel in Griffith Park.

In the amazing Forest Lawn Memorial Cemetery in Glendale, whose Slumberland, Whispering Pines and replicas of the Wee Kirk o' the Heather and de Vinci's *Last Supper* were satirized in Waugh's *The Loved Ones,* and Disneyland, the superb playground for children and adults at Anaheim, L.A. has two of America's best-known attractions.

Yet, despite their size and significance, neither Los Angeles nor San Francisco is the state capital. That honor belongs to Sacramento, the cradle of California, where Marshall, the carpenter at Sutter's Sawmill, picked up the state's future on that rainy day in 1884. Sacramento's Capitol Building, housing the State legislature, was built in 1861 and its archives and library hold in their files the enthralling and dramatic history of California.

When asked a few years ago what California had to offer, a state government official made the following points: an unmatched educational system allowing greater economic opportunity; newer buildings, therefore better houses and offices; and the best system of highways in the United States.

Educational facilities are almost unparalleled. The state pumps in well over 700 million dollars in funds to the educational system which, at the higher level, was hugely expanded in the 1960s. The existing University of California campuses at Berkeley (perhaps the most prestigious of them, founded in 1868), Los Angeles, Davis Riverside, Santa Barbara and San Francisco were supplemented by new sites at Irvine, Santa Cruz and San Diego. The California university system has produced many notable academics and is proud of the many Nobel Prize winners on its faculties. It houses two nuclear research laboratories, nearly 100 research and experimental stations and in many fields of endeavor – particularly medicine, science and biology – is in the forefront of world research.

As the state moved into the 1970s it had over 14 million registered vehicles, the greatest concentration in the world. To cope with this mobile army there were nearly 4,000 miles of multi-lane freeways and it was possible to drive north for 500 miles from San Diego on free motorways without having to stop for a traffic light or intersection.

California life as practiced, as eulogized in song and on film, is one of perpetual motion. The Californian moves home and travels in the course of business and pleasure far more than any other American. And in a city like Los Angeles, which covers such a huge area and in which public transport plays such a minor part, an automobile is absolutely essential.

But this brings its own problems. "By the early 1980s," Michael Davie reported one authority as saying, "we'll have 20 million cars. We've already got 14 million. I've got three myself: one for me, one for my wife, one for my son. It's out of control. You know they even want to put a freeway through one of the national parks..."

So, as California, the pioneer of new lifestyles, forges through the 1980s, the voice of protest against rapid change is growing – against freeways, pollution, high technology and a multitude of other subjects. At risk, it says, is the very quality of life.

This growing feeling has spawned, over the recent past, a rash of cults and sects: theosophists, followers of Krishnamurti, Rosicrucians, the Beat Generation, Hippies, Zen Buddhists, creeds based on the occult, on faith healing, rock music, drugs and communes.

It is as if, after years of leading the world in experimentation, Californians are seeking to pause for breath, to take stock of their lives, to seek new solutions to new problems.

The state is aware of these feelings; almost every week there is legislative action of some kind dealing with energy, water, land use – all issues that have a major bearing on the quality of life.

And to ensure that the state does not forget its responsibilities, pressure groups – nearly 600 concerned with the environment alone – are active on all the major issues, the chief of which is whether and how the land should be used or changed, and for whose benefit.

On their past record, Californians have the ability and the resources to deal with their problems; to move into a new era like the one that began all those years ago at Sutter's Mill.

Facing page: San Diego's Hotel del Coronado.

Previous pages: two views of central San Diego, an important port and military base with a total population of over a million. Balboa Park (these pages) is a 1,100-acre park in the heart of San Diego and contains such buildings as the House of Pacific Relations (above) and the Casas del Prado (facing page). Overleaf: (left) North Harbor Island and (right) a golf course on the Coronado Peninsula.

Facing page: Seaport Village, a shopping area on the junction of Harbor Drive and Pacific Highway. Above: the Japanese Village in Seaworld, where divers demonstrate the harvesting of pearls. Overleaf: aerial views of central San Diego.

These pages: the downtown area where Harbor Drive runs alongside San Diego Bay is famed for its fine seafood restaurants. Overleaf: (left) the graceful sweep of the San Diego Coronado Bay Bridge and (right) the low buildings of the Coronado Peninsula.

Previous pages: the Church of the Immaculate Conception (left) in San Diego's Old Town and (right) Seaport Village. Facing page: the magnificent, red-roofed Hotel del Coronado was constructed in 1887 and has maintained its pre-eminence ever since. Above: the San Diego Coronado Bay Bridge. Overleaf: (left) yachts moored in Glorietta Bay and (right) houses on the Coronado Peninsula.

Previous pages: (left) yachts on San Diego Bay and (right) Mission San Diego de Alcalá, founded in 1774 and still functioning as a parish church. Above: the surf of the Pacific and the sheltered waters of Mission Bay from the north. Facing page: Mission Boulevard and Mission Bay. Overleaf: La Jolla, with (right) the curved breakwater of Children's Pool.

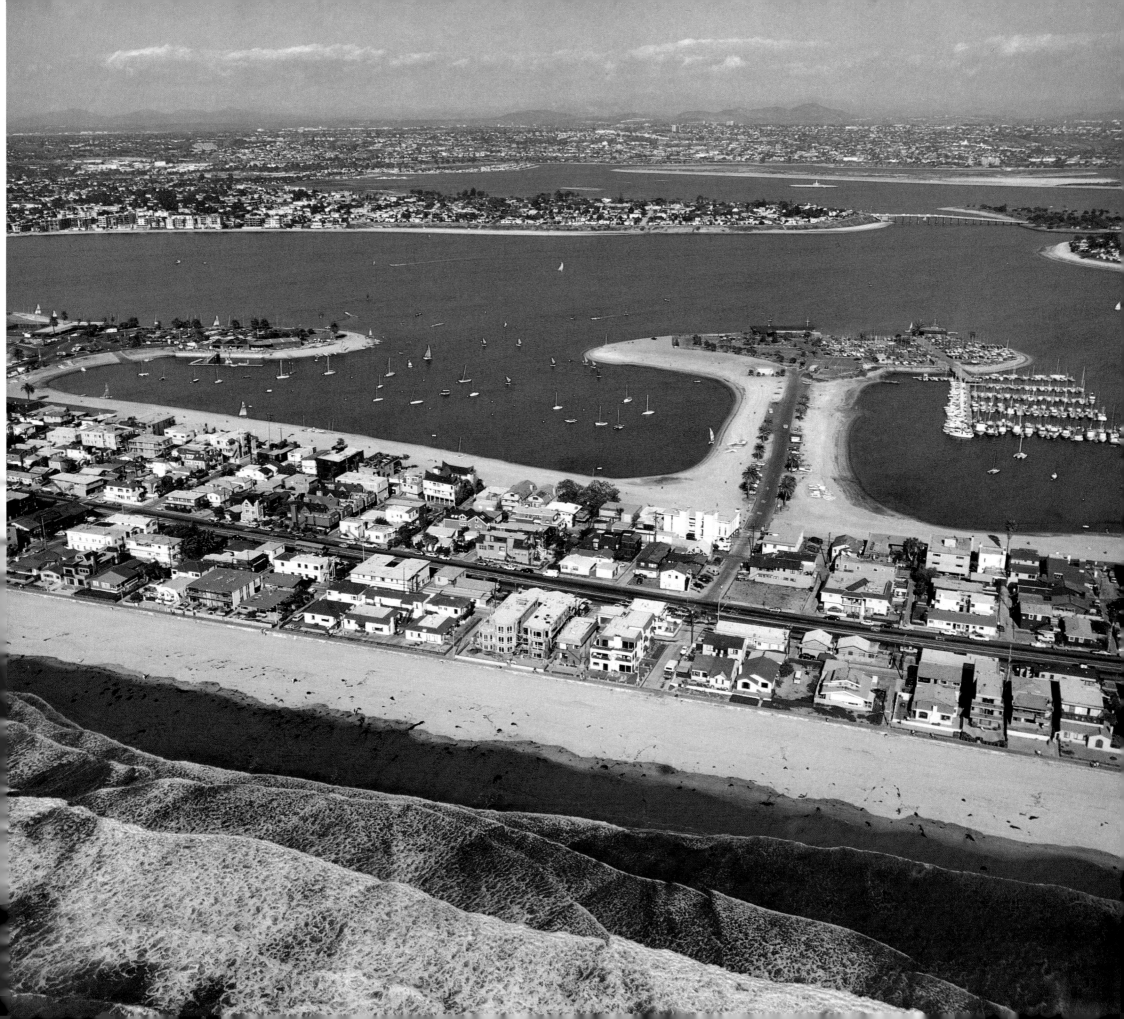

La Jolla (these pages and overleaf) is officially part of San Diego, but it lies some miles to the north and
retains its distinctive character. Its name derives from one of two Spanish words, meaning either 'a jewel' or
'a pit', local pride usually declares the former to be the correct derivation. Above: Children's Pool.

North and east of Indio lie the 870 square miles of Joshua Tree National Monument (above) where many types of desert life can be found. Facing page: the Palm Spring Aerial Tramway, which takes visitors up to 8,500 feet and affords fine views of the San Jacinto Mountains. Overleaf: (left) the Living Desert Reserve near Palm Springs and (right) the Anza-Borrego State Park.

The beautiful and varied coast of California is one of the most diverse in the world. Above: the hills around
Avila Beach, near Santa Barbara, and (facing page) the low land backing Newport Beach.

When Juan Rodriguez Cabrillo sighted the land that would become San Diego in 1542, the great Pacific rollers
had been smashing against the shore for millions of years. Where the pounding waves meet the land they have
carved many strange rock formations, as at Windansea Beach (facing page) and Bird Rock (above). Overleaf: Long
Beach, with (left) Whalers Wharf and (right) the *Queen Mary*.

Above: yachts moored in a marina at Long Beach. Facing page: the Union Bank Building and the gleaming Bonaventure Hotel, Los Angeles. Overleaf: (left) Century Plaza and (right) the Hotel Beverly Wilshire, both in Los Angeles.

Marina del Rey is perhaps best known for the area known as Fisherman's Village (these pages), on Fiji Way. The cobblestoned streets and Cape Cod-style buildings cluster around the 60-foot-tall lighthouse (below and right). Overleaf: (left) Los Angeles City Hall and (right) the Triforium, focal point of Los Angeles Mall.

Los Angeles. Above: the luxurious and modern Bonaventure Hotel on 5th Street. Facing page: central Los Angeles from the southwest. Overleaf: (left) flamingos at Los Angeles Zoo and (right) Mann's Chinese Theater and other sights along Hollywood Boulevard.

61

Above: the sheer, reflective wall of a building in downtown Los Angeles. Facing page: Los Angeles' magnificent
Memorial Coliseum, which was built in 1932 to host the 10th Olympiad and hosted the Olympics again in 1984.
Overleaf: New Year celebrations in Los Angeles' Chinatown.

62

Above: central Los Angeles from the southwest. Facing page: the Harbor Freeway curves around the city.
Overleaf: (left) Marineland, which features daily shows of killer whales, dolphins and sea lions, and (right) Beverly Hills City Hall.

Above: the Hyatt Hotel in Long Beach. Facing page: some of the glittering, modern facades of downtown Los Angeles. Overleaf: (left) a memorial to Thomas Jefferson in Woodlawn Cemetery and (right) the Los Angeles Memorial Sports Hall.

Between Santa Monica and Marina del Rey is Venice Boulevard, a hive of activity with its many stalls and fast-food outlets (left, far left and below left). Below: The Cookie House, on the beach at Santa Monica. Within the borders of the Los Angeles State and County Arboretum (facing page) can be found four interesting and historic buildings and several specialised gardens with fascinating, exotic plants. Overleaf: (left) the luxury, 300-room Beverly Hills Hotel and (right) central Los Angeles.

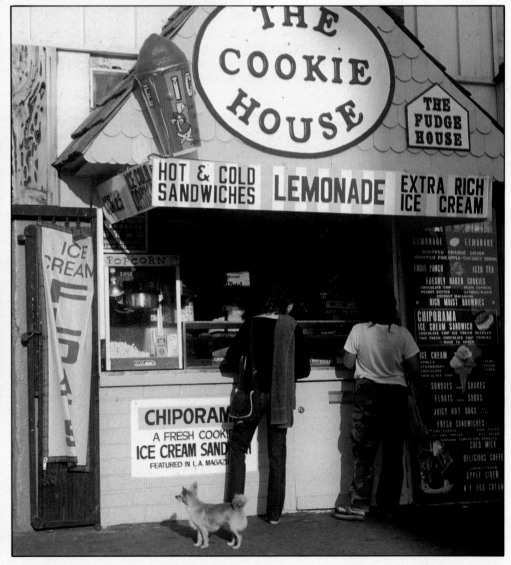

Shopping is always an experience in Los Angeles, especially on Olvera Street (this page and facing page, top left, top right and bottom right), where the Mexican influence is strongest. Farmers Market (facing page bottom left), off Fairfax Avenue, sells a wide variety of goods. Overleaf: the 87-acre South Coast Botanic Gardens, which contain more than 2,000 species of plants.

Los Angeles. Above: the pier at Moby's Dock. Facing page: the reflecting wall of a downtown building.

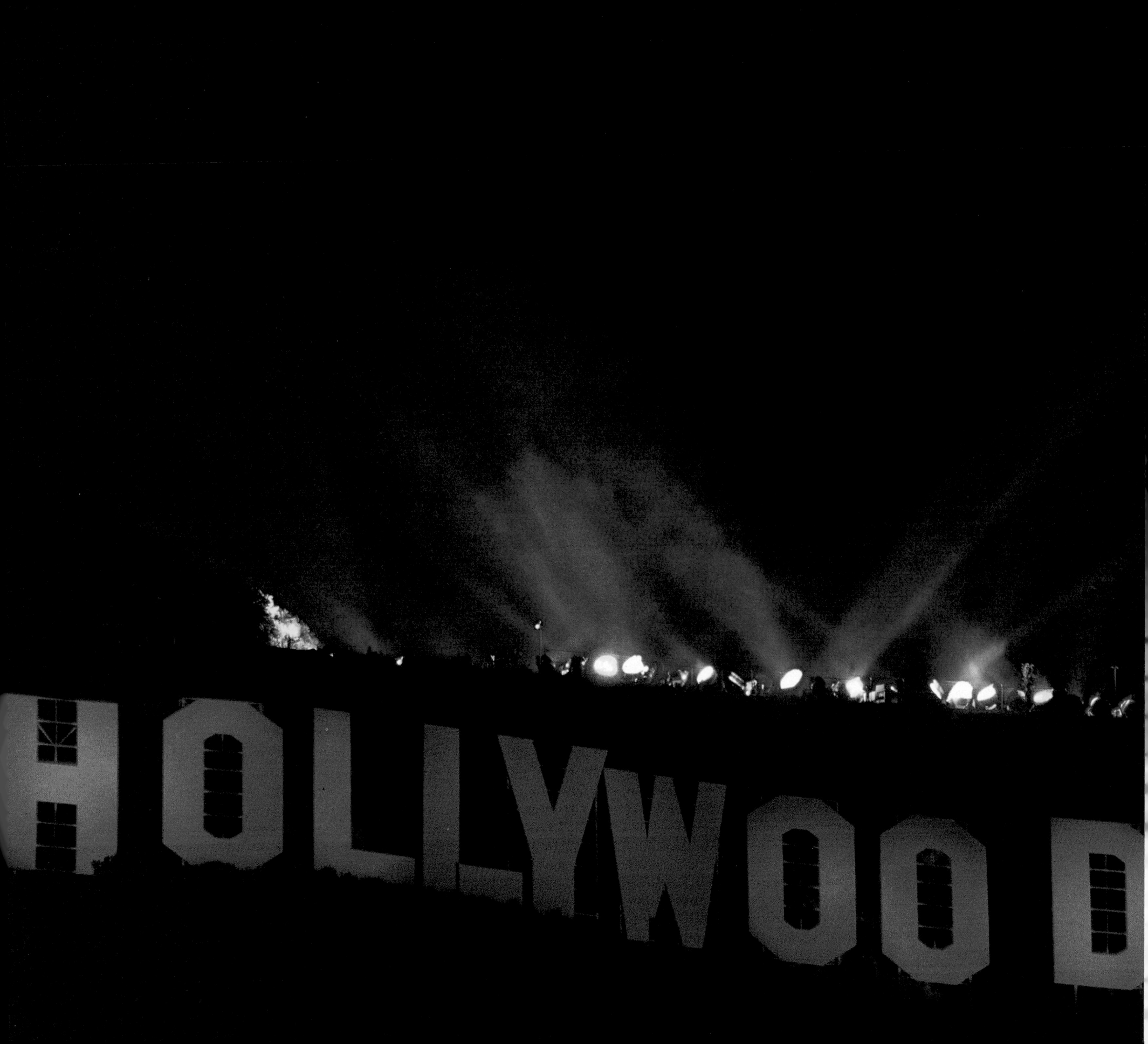
HOLLYWOOD

Facing page: the famous 45-foot-tall letters that stand above Hollywood were erected in 1928 and refurbished in 1978. Above: a view from Los Angeles Port Scenic Drive. Overleaf: (left) the natural amphitheater of the Hollywood Bowl, home of the Los Angeles Philharmonic Orchestra, and (right) the Universal Studios.

These pages: some of the magnificent mansions around Beverly Hills. Overleaf: Santa Monica, a town within the Los Angeles city limits, known for its clear air and relaxing atmosphere.

These pages and overleaf right: the broad sweep of sand which has made Santa Monica such a popular place for Los Angelenos intent on swimming or sun-bathing. Overleaf: (left) the palm-fringed sands of Venice, another coastal town now swallowed up by Los Angeles.

These pages: dusk gathers over the beach at Santa Monica. Overleaf: (left) the well-posted Pepperdine University, near Malibu, and (right) the J. Paul Getty Museum, built in the style of an ancient Roman villa, where many Baroque and more modern works of art are on show.

These pages: the golden sands of Pacific Palisades, where an engineered stream reaches the sea and has its course changed dramatically by natural deposition of sand. Overleaf: (left) Santa Barbara and (right) the beach at Malibu.

These pages and overleaf: the dramatically-varied and inhospitable scenery of Death Valley, the lowest valley in the nation, reaching 282 feet below sea level. The valley was formed when a huge block of rock, some 120 miles long, was surrounded by massive faults and slipped downwards while surrounding mountains rose up.

These pages: Pfeiffer Beach is located just south of the entrance to Pfeiffer-Big Sur State Park and is approached along the narrow Sycamore Canyon Road. Overleaf: (left) a magnificent, colonnaded swimming pool at San Simeon, the fabulous, one-time home of William Randolph Hearst, and (right) Bixby Creek Bridge, south of Carmel.

Previous pages: (left) Bixby Creek Bridge and (right) a view southward toward Big Sur. These pages: Big Sur and Monterey Peninsula's coastlines are studded with crags and rocks which have proven to be the ruin of many a ship on its way to safe harbor in Monterey Bay. Overleaf: (left) Limekiln Beach and (right) Piedras Blancas, both around Big Sur.

Above: black and heavy storm clouds blot out the sun's rays at Point Sur. Facing page: the sun bejewels the sea at China Cove, the only safe swimming beach in Point Lobos State Reserve. Overleaf: the Carmel River State Beach, which attracts people from far and wide with its sandy shore and picturesque surroundings.

These pages: two idyllic beaches on the rugged Big Sur coastline, (facing page) at Mill Creek and (above) at Julia Pfeiffer-Burns Park. Overleaf: the romantic, rock-strewn shoreline of Carmel River State Beach touched by the setting sun.

Looping west from Pacific Grove is one of the most scenically-impressive stretches of road in California. The famed 17-mile Drive runs around the Monterey Peninsula to take in such sights as Cypress Point (previous pages left) and the rock-strewn headland (previous pages right). The drive ends at Carmel, where Pacific rollers crash to shore in a welter of spray (these pages). Overleaf: Point Lobos.

Facing page: Gray Whale Cove, north of Montara, with its unspoilt beach. Above: Point Lobos State Reserve, whose famous stands of Monterey Cypress are pictured (overleaf). This cypress, known scientifically as *Cupressus macrocarpa*, has wood which is hard and resistant, but its use is limited by its unpleasant odor.

Facing page: a rare sea otter in its characteristic sleeping posture, floating on its back and wrapped in a strand of kelp. Above: a seal with her pup. Overleaf: the Pebble Beach golf course on Monterey Peninsula, one of the most beautifully-sited courses in California.

These pages: the town of Monterey, which was chosen by the Spaniards as the capital of Alta California. The commercial fishing boats which kept the town busy for half a century have now been replaced by the pleasure craft which crowd the bay and marina, while Fisherman's Wharf (above) has gained shops, an art gallery and a theater. Overleaf: a carpet of mauve blooms covers Lovers' Point at Pacific Grove.

Previous pages left and overleaf right: the huge sequoias are the most sought after and popular features of Kings Canyon National Park, east of Fresno, but the tumbling waters (above and overleaf left) which carve the canyon have a beauty all their own. Previous pages right: the sheer walls of The Sentinel. Facing page: the dramatic scenery around Horseshoe Road.

Yosemite National Park (these pages and overleaf) is one of the most spectacular areas in California: (above) the Upper Yosemite Falls; (facing page) the view from the mouth of the Wawona Tunnel; (overleaf left) the cascading Vernal Falls and (overleaf right) sunset gleams on the face of Half Dome as it stands above the valley.

Yosemite National Park: (facing page) El Capitan and the Merced River; (above) the distinctive face of Half Dome from the banks of the tranquil Merced River; (overleaf left) Cathedral Rocks and (overleaf right) the Upper and Lower Yosemite Falls.

Above: the crumbling wooden buildings of Bodie State Historic Park, once one of the toughest gold-mining towns in the West. Facing page: the Dana River in the spring, tumbling seawards with its load of melted snow. Overleaf: (left) a car stirs up dust in Sonora Pass, one of the routes near Bridgeport which is often closed by winter snows, and (right) a cattle ranch north of Bridgeport, near the Nevada border.

Above: a melt-water stream in the Sierra Nevada. Facing page: Mono Lake and surrounding peaks near Bridgeport.
Overleaf: (left) fishermen on the still surface of Silver Lake, in the High Sierras, and (right) a cowboy and
his horse pick their way through the High Sierras.

Above and top: the ten-block section of Old Sacramento, which has been restored and renovated in keeping with its gold rush origins. Top left and left: Capitol Mall. Facing page: the Capitol from the air. Overleaf: (left) the interior of the Capitol dome and (right) the Capitol.

Previous pages: (top left) the Firehouse; (bottom left) Broad Street and (right hand page) Main Street, all in Nevada City; (top center) Old City Hall and (top right) the Firehouse in Auburn; (bottom right) the Empire Mine, Grass Valley. Facing page: a ship on the canal near Sacramento. Above: grain fields in the Delta Valley.

173

Facing page: farmland near Livermore. This page and overleaf: scenes near Yuba City; (top left, top right and overleaf left) the rich grain harvest; (above) a plaque in the Sutter Buttes; (right) thinning peaches in the orchards and (overleaf right) grazing land east of Yuba City.

San Francisco is arguably the greatest city on the West Coast, drawing its strength from its many-faceted cultural scene as well as its economic and commercial power. Above and overleaf: the San Francisco-Oakland Bay Bridge, which was completed in 1937 and runs for some eight miles across San Francisco Bay. Facing page: the open Pacific beyond Golden Gate Bridge.

Previous pages: (left) bay windows on some of the older houses in San Francisco and (right) gabled houses on Steiner Street. Above: the columned Palace of the Fine Arts, built in 1915 for the World's Fair. Facing page: the clock tower of the Ferry Building and nearby wharves. Overleaf: a panorama of the city looking west from Battery Street.

Facing page: Downtown San Francisco, seen from Mission Dolores Park, towers over the predominantly Latin area to the south. Above and overleaf: Telegraph Hill and Coit Tower, which was built in 1934 by Mrs. Lillie Coit as a memorial to the firefighters of the city.

Previous pages: the Embarcadero Skyway and downtown San Francisco. Facing page: the Renaissance-style dome of City Hall, constructed to replace that destroyed during the earthquake of 1906. Above: the Palace of Fine Arts, designed by Bernard Maybeck as a temporary structure, has proved its permanence and has only needed strengthening in recent years. Overleaf: the San Francisco-Oakland Bay Bridge and downtown San Francisco.

Facing page: the city center and the San Francisco-Oakland Bay Bridge. Above: a merchant ship steams beneath the Golden Gate Bridge. Overleaf: (left) Grant Avenue in San Francisco's Chinatown area and (right) the very steep and winding Lombard Street, whose course was dictated by the rigid grid system of the city streets.

Previous pages: the Palace of Fine Arts and Golden Gate Bridge. Facing page: the elegant, Gothic-style Lone Mountain Campus of the University of San Francisco. Above: one of the many parks which grace San Francisco. Overleaf: the colorful sights of Chinatown, where Oriental shops and restaurants crowd the streets and the largest Chinese community outside Asia finds its home.

Above: the Coit Tower and central San Francisco. Facing page: a magnificent view of the Golden Gate and its famous bridge. Overleaf: (left) the Golden Gate Bridge, shrouded by the mist which often creeps into the Bay in the summer months, and (right) Steiner Street at night.

Above: the distinctive shape of the towering Trans America Pyramid punctures the evening skyline of San Francisco. Facing page: the Golden Gate Bridge at night. Overleaf: a view across the city center towards the Golden Gate.

Alcatraz Island (these pages) first served as a military base in the 1850s and then saw service as a prison for Apaches in the 1870s before becoming a federal prison. The harsh regime and impossibility of escape made the island notorious, but the prison was closed in 1963 and the crumbling buildings are now a tourist attraction. Overleaf: the city center from above the Golden Gate.

Above: the World Trade Center and the Ferry Building, constructed in 1896 in the style of the cathedral in Seville, in Spain. Facing page: the huge, 750-foot-tall towers which support the Golden Gate Bridge. Overleaf: a residential area of the city.

Previous pages: (left) gabled houses in Steiner Street and (right) boats moored at Fisherman's Wharf, where many fine seafood restaurants are to be found. Facing page: the modern skyline of San Francisco. Above: a cargo ship passes beneath the Golden Gate Bridge. Overleaf: some of the well-preserved older houses of the city, showing the preference for bay windows in years gone by.

In 1579 Sir Francis Drake landed on a coast he called New Albion and which he claimed for Elizabeth I of England. Just where he landed has long been disputed, but it is believed to have been in the region of Point Reyes National Seashore: (above) the Point Reyes Lighthouse and (facing page) the view from Chimney Rock. Overleaf: (left) Bodega Bay, an active fishing port west of Santa Rosa, and (right) the Sonoma coast.

Previous pages: landscapes around Healdsburg. Above: Smugglers Cove, north of Gualala. Facing page: the picturesque, rocky shore of Salt Point. Overleaf: (left) Clear Lake near Konocti; (top center) a lifeguard by Clear Lake; (bottom center) Port Sonoma Marina; (top right) Clear Lake State Park and (bottom right) Lake Mendocino.

ATTENTION PUBLIC

LIFEGUARD ON DUTY
AT THIS BEACH FROM
10 A.M. TO 6 P.M. DAILY

PARK COMMISSIONER CITY OF LAKEPORT

NO SWIMMING
OR
DIVING
FROM
PIERS OR FLOATS

243

Facing page: driftwood scattered along the sands at Elk Cove, north of Elk. Above: the thin trickle of water that is Elk Creek runs over the sands to reach the Pacific, south of Mendocino. Overleaf: (left) the Burl Sculpture at Benbow; (center) the huge Chandelier redwood near Leggett and (right) the sun sinks below the Pacific horizon south of Eureka.

Above and overleaf right: yachts and working vessels moored in the Woodly Island Marina in Eureka, the most important port between San Francisco and the Columbia River. Facing page: 2nd Street in Eureka. Overleaf left: the small building which serves as the lighthouse at Trinidad, north of Eureka.

Previous pages: (left) the Klamath River in turbulent mood and (right) a truck carries logs across the river
near Weitchpec. Above: a view from the Klamath Overlook. Facing page: two examples of the massive redwoods
near Klamath. Overleaf: (left) Point St. George, just ten miles south of the Oregon state line and (right)
part of the two mile row of fishermen's campers which borders United States Highway 101 south of Klamath.

BIG TREE
HEIGHT   304   92.6
DIAMETER   21.8   6.6
CIRCUMFERENCE 68   20.7
ESTIMATED AGE   1500 YRS.

SHRINE
DRIVE-THRU TREE
AGE 5000   HEIGHT 275 FT.
21   CIR. 64 FT.
MYERS FLAT, CALIFORNIA

Top left: Christian Brothers Vineyard, (above) Berlinger Brothers Vineyard and (top right and overleaf left) nearby scenes, all around St. Helena. Left: the home of General Mariano Guadalupe Vallejo, founder of Sonora. Facing page and overleaf right: vineyards near Healdsburg.

234

Above: coastal fog rolls in among the redwoods at sunset. Facing page and overleaf left: the Ladybird Johnson Grove of coast redwoods, the tallest living things in the world. Overleaf right: a coastal fog rolls in towards the mountains in Redwood National Park.

Above: an automatic irrigation device waters fields near Tule Lake. Facing page: the boulder-strewn bed of Gumboot Creek. Overleaf: (left) a lone catamaran on the waters of Lake Siskiyou and (right) a dead tree at the Lava Beds National Monument, near Tule Lake.

Previous pages left and these pages: the 14,161-foot-high mass of Mount Shasta rises above the countryside north of Redding. Previous pages right: the impressive heights of Castle Crags, which lie south of Dunsmuir. The crags were formed out of 200-million-year-old granite by the forces of erosion and given their final shaping during the Ice Ages in the last million years. Overleaf: Lake Shasta.

Top left: the Glory Hole and (remaining pictures) the magnificent beach at Brandy Creek, both at Whiskeytown Reservoir, west of Redding. Overleaf: (left) the Camden House, near Redding, built in 1852 by Charles Camden, and (right) boats in the Brandy Creek Marina on Whiskeytown Reservoir.

Facing page: the incredibly delicate tracery of the Burnley Falls, east of Enterprise. Above: the forest and grazing land of the Mount Shasta-Fall River area. Overleaf: (left) the road curving beneath Mount Lassen and (right) Boiling Lake in Bumpass Hell, both in Lassen Volcanic National Park.

Lassen Volcanic National Park. These pages: the steaming springs and lakes of Bumpass Hell reveal the recent volcanic history of the area. Overleaf: (left) a tumbling stream near the Sulfur Works Thermal Area and (right) snow-spattered Mount Conrad.

Between 1914 and 1921 a series of eruptions occured at Lassen Peak in northeastern California, though today the volcano has settled down somewhat. Lassen Volcanic Park covers some 163 square miles around the peak and includes gushing streams such as Hat Creek (above) and thermal areas such as Bumpass Hell (overleaf). Facing page: the Painted Dunes.

DANGER
MUD POTS, FUMAROLES
AND POOLS ARE VERY HOT
GROUND CRUST MAY BE
THIN OR SLIPPERY
STAY ON TRAILS

Lake Tahoe. Previous pages: (left) picnickers at Eldorado Beach and (right) yachts moored in a marina at Tahoe Keys, on the south shore of the lake. Above and overleaf left: the sandy beach of D.L. Bliss State Park, a 1,237-acre reserve of forested mountainside overlooking the lake. Facing page: the *Tahoe Queen* takes on passengers at South Lake Tahoe. Overleaf right: the Olympic Valley Inn, north of D.L. Bliss State Park.

Lake Tahoe. Above: the emerald surface of Lake Tahoe at sandy Eldorado Beach. Facing page: the *Tahoe Queen* in Emerald Bay. Overleaf: (left) trees and undergrowth cling precariously to the rugged mountain slopes above Emerald Bay and (right) small craft on the sandy beach at South Lake Tahoe.

Lake Tahoe. Facing page: the clear waters of Lake Tahoe at D.L. Bliss State Park. Above and overleaf: the picturesque beauty of the ruin-topped Fannette Island in Emerald Bay, perhaps the most scenic part of Lake Tahoe, an area noted for its beauty and one of the foremost mountain resorts in the state.

Lake Tahoe. These pages: Fannette Island and Emerald Bay from the surrounding heights.

INDEX